D1313867

$20.00

DOG BREEDS

Poodles

by Mari Schuh

Consultant:
Michael Leuthner, D.V.M.
PetCare Clinic, Madison, Wisc.

BLASTOFF! READERS
4

BELLWETHER MEDIA · MINNEAPOLIS, MN

Note to Librarians, Teachers, and Parents:

Blastoff! Readers are carefully developed by literacy experts and combine standards-based content with developmentally appropriate text.

Level 1 provides the most support through repetition of high-frequency words, light text, predictable sentence patterns, and strong visual support.

Level 2 offers early readers a bit more challenge through varied simple sentences, increased text load, and less repetition of high-frequency words.

Level 3 advances early-fluent readers toward fluency through increased text and concept load, less reliance on visuals, longer sentences, and more literary language.

Level 4 builds reading stamina by providing more text per page, increased use of punctuation, greater variation in sentence patterns, and increasingly challenging vocabulary.

Level 5 encourages children to move from "learning to read" to "reading to learn" by providing even more text, varied writing styles, and less familiar topics.

Whichever book is right for your reader, Blastoff! Readers are the perfect books to build confidence and encourage a love of reading that will last a lifetime!

This edition first published in 2009 by Bellwether Media.

No part of this publication may be reproduced in whole or in part without written permission of the publisher. For information regarding permission, write to Bellwether Media Inc., Attention: Permissions Department, Post Office Box 19349, Minneapolis, MN 55419-0349.

Library of Congress Cataloging-in-Publication Data
Schuh, Mari C., 1975-
  Poodles / by Mari Schuh.
    p. cm. — (Blastoff! readers. Dog breeds)
  Includes bibliographical references and index.
  Summary: "Simple text and full color photographs introduce beginning readers to the characteristics of the dog breed Poodles . Developed by literacy experts for students in kindergarten through third grade"—Provided by publisher.
  ISBN-13: 978-1-60014-220-8 (hardcover : alk. paper)
  ISBN-10: 1-60014-220-6 (hardcover : alk. paper)
  1. Poodles—Juvenile literature. I. Title.

SF429.P85S38 2009
636.72'8—dc22
                                          2008020004

Contents

What Are Poodles?

Poodles are a **breed** of dog with fluffy, curly hair. Some Poodle owners give their dogs fancy haircuts. Others let the hair grow long.

The **coat** of most Poodles is one solid color. It can be white, black, brown, gray, or cream-colored. It can also be a shade of orange called apricot.

Poodles come in three sizes. They are
Standard, Toy, and Miniature. Standard
Poodles are the biggest size. They are more
than 15 inches (38 centimeters) tall at the
shoulder. They weigh between 45 and 70
pounds (20.4 and 31.8 kilograms).

Toy Poodles are the smallest. They are 10 inches (25.4 centimeters) or shorter at their shoulder. They weigh between 3 and 4 pounds (1.4 and 1.8 kilograms).

Poodles are one of the longest-
living dog breeds. Many Poodles
live into their mid-teen or late-teen
years. Among Poodles, Miniature
Poodles live the longest.

Miniature Poodles are the middle size.
They are between 11 and 15 inches
(28 and 38.1 centimeters) tall at their
shoulders. They weigh between 15 and
17 pounds (6.8 and 7.7 kilograms).

Poodles have long front legs that are thin and straight. Strong, thick hind legs help them run and swim. Poodles have a long, straight **muzzle** and floppy ears. They have a strong neck and dark, oval eyes.

History of Poodles

No one knows exactly how the Poodle breed began, but they have been around for a long time. The Toy Poodle was in England about 300 years ago. A German artist drew pictures of Poodles nearly 600 years ago.

Most people believe that Poodles came from Germany. The dogs were used as hunting dogs to retrieve prey. Poodles may have also been used to **herd** animals.

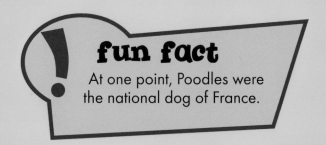

fun fact

At one point, Poodles were the national dog of France.

The name *Poodle* has a German origin. It comes from the German word *Pudelhund*. In German, *Pudel* means "puddle" and *Hund* means "dog." The word *Pudelhund* means "splashing dog." This means that Poodles were likely used as **water retrievers** in Germany.

fun fact

The first Toy Poodles that existed were almost always white. Toy Poodles were then bred with colored Miniature Poodles so that Toy Poodles would be different colors.

Poodles did not swim in deep rivers and lakes. Poodles retrieved prey in marshes and swamps. They splashed in shallow water.

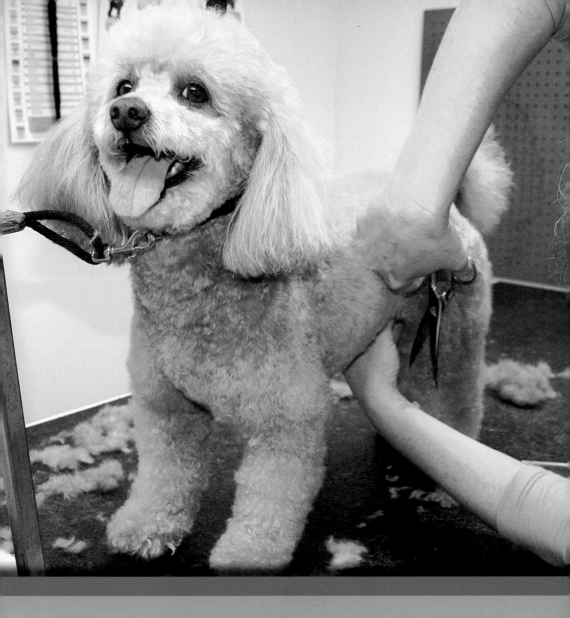

Owners cut the hair of Poodles to make it easier for the dogs to get through water. Some areas of the dog were left covered to keep Poodles warm in cold water.

Some Poodles in Europe hunted for **truffles**. Truffles are a rare **fungus** that some people enjoy eating. The Poodles sniffed for and dug up this expensive food.

Poodles have had other jobs as well. Some worked as guard dogs. Others performed in circuses.

Poodles Today

Poodles are active dogs with lots of energy. They compete in many kinds of dog events. In **agility** events, Poodles run through obstacle courses as fast as they can. In **tracking** events, they follow **scent trails** to try and find a lost object or person.

Many Poodles compete in dog shows. Judges rate them on how they look compared to the other dogs.

Poodles can make great pets. Most are eager to please, easy to train, and love to be with people. Poodles find a place in many homes around the world.

fun fact

In the 1950s, many young American girls wore poodle skirts. These wide skirts were very popular. They featured a Poodle design on the front.

Glossary

agility—a dog sport where dogs run through a series of obstacles

breed—a type of dog

coat—the hair or fur of an animal

fungus—a kind of living thing; types of fungi include mushrooms, yeasts, molds, and truffles.

herd—to make people or animals move as a group

muzzle—the nose, jaws, and mouth of an animal

scent trails—smells that animals or people leave behind as they travel

tracking—a dog sport where dogs track scent trails

truffle—an expensive fungus that some people enjoy eating

water retriever—a dog that gets something and brings it back from the water; water retrievers fetch prey such as wild ducks from rivers, marshes, and swamps.

To Learn More

AT THE LIBRARY

Fitzpatrick, Anne. *Poodles*. Mankato, Minn.: Smart Apple Media, 2003.

MacAulay, Kelley and Bobbie Kalman. *Poodles*. New York: Crabtree, 2007.

Trumbauer, Lisa. *Poodles*. Mankato, Minn.: Capstone, 2006.

ON THE WEB

Learning more about Poodles is as easy as 1, 2, 3.

1. Go to www.factsurfer.com

2. Enter "Poodles" into search box.

3. Click the "Surf" button and you will see a list of related web sites.

With factsurfer.com, finding more information is just a click away.

Index

The images in this book are reproduced through the courtesy of: Lee Feldstein, front cover;
Pix 'n Pages, pp. 4, 17; Tootles, p. 5; Shershel / Dreamstime, p. 6; AFP / Getty Images, p. 7;
DC / Photolink Ltd / Alamy, p. 8; JUNIORS BILDARCHIV / age fotostock, pp. 9, 13, 20;
Fernando Soares, pp. 10-11; Mark Raycroft / Getty Images, pp. 14, 16; Jana Lumley, p. 15;
Daniel Dempster Photography / Alamy, pp. 18-19.